CW00645883

IN SEARCH OF GOD

QUANTUM PHYSICS

IN SEARCH OF GOD

QUANTUM PHYSICS

No element of this publication may be reproduced, stored in a retrieval system, nor transmitted in any form or means without either the prior written permission of the publisher or author. This includes electronic, mechanical, photocopying, recording, scanning, or otherwise; except as permitted under Section 107 or 108 of the 1976 United States Copyright Act. Requests to the publisher for reprint permission should be addressed to:

Author: Dr. CK Quarterman
131 Franklin Plaza, Suite 204
Franklin, NC 28734

ISBN-13:
978-1518866371

ISBN-10:
1518866379

Quotations are from the King James Version of the Bible unless otherwise noted.

Printed in the United States of America.

Contents

Prologue

In Romans we are told that,

"For the invisible things of him from the creation of the world are clearly seen, being understood by the things that are made, even his eternal power and Godhead; so that they are without excuse: "(Rom 1:20)

So the thought occurred to me to prove the truthfulness and reliability of intelligent design and that there is a Creator and that He is the God of the Bible by looking at the invisible world of Quantum physics.

It is in this world of Quantum Physics (of orderly, set laws) into which I want to give you a glimpse everything in this world acts in an orderly way. There is no disorder, no chaos. Everything acts according to set laws. The quantum world is a microscopic world where everything has a purpose and an order. We will talk a lot about Uranium whose half-life is longer than the age of the Earth. The half-life of uranium is about 4.47 billion years. So it is clear that the laws effecting quantum physics have not "evolved" over time, but were set in their bounds by the creator. Hence, we can be sure that mankind didn't evolve over time, but was created by the God of the Bible.

> *The LORD by wisdom hath founded the earth; by understanding hath he established the heavens.* (Pro 3:19)

Intelligent design

"Intelligent design states that, "certain features of the universe and of living things are best explained by an intelligent cause, not an undirected process such as natural selection".

I am going to prove to you that the laws of Quantum physics show intelligent cause. Further that it is the God of the Bible who has directed the design. I am going to do this by showing the design of atoms and how they function using the best known example of the atom, the atom bomb. I am going to show you the laws which govern subatomic particles and demonstrate that they couldn't have just "evolved". My assertions are that the laws by which Quantum physics operate are far too complex and predictable to have merely happened by chance.

The essential argument for design is that highly complex phenomena (such Quantum physics) demonstrate the direct action of the hand of God. The appearance of complexity in nature cannot be explained through natural causes; it requires the guidance of an "intelligent agent," God himself.

"Whether a supernatural force does or does not act is thus outside of what science can tell us". (Scott 1998)

I disagree; if those forces were created billions of years ago, I think that would show a supernatural force working within so called science. I will be showing some of these scriptures as we go that prove God knew (before the world began) of the forces that control atoms before the world began and that He put them in place.

Quantum physics

Quantum physics is the study of the discrete units of matter and energy that are predicted by and observed by quantum physics. In the realm of quantum physics, matter can go from one spot to another without moving through the intervening space. Observing the interaction actually influences the physical processes taking place. An essential feature of quantum mechanics is that it is generally impossible, even in principle, to measure a system without disturbing it. Quantum physics is sometimes called *quantum mechanics*. More accurately it is a fundamental branch of physics that deals with physical phenomena at a nanoscopic level, where the action is on the order of the Planck constant.

Planck constant E=hv. Equivalently, the smallness of the Planck constant reflects the fact that everyday objects and systems are made of a *large* number of particles. The planck is the shortest measurable length. No theoretically known improvement in measurements or instrumentation can change that. Max Planck discovered in 1900 that you couldn't get smaller than a certain minimum amount of anything.

This minimum amount is now called the Planck unit. The mathematical formulations of quantum mechanics are abstract so I won't write much about the mathematical functions or of probability which require complex numbers and linear functions.

Quantum mechanics is essential to understanding the behavior of atoms. Electrons remain in an uncertain, non-deterministic, probabilistic wave–particle orbital about the nucleus, defying the traditional assumptions of classical mechanics and electromagnetism. Thus quantum mechanics was initially developed to provide a better explanation and description of the atom. If the physical nature of an atom was solely described by classical mechanics, electrons would not orbit the nucleus, since orbiting electrons emit radiation (due to circular motion) and would eventually collide with the nucleus due to this loss of energy. Classical mechanics is unable to explain the stability of atoms. Contrary to classical mechanics, one can never make simultaneous predictions of variables, such as position and momentum, with accuracy. For instance, electrons may be considered to be located somewhere within a given region of space, but with their exact positions unknown. Contours of constant probability, often referred to as "clouds", may be drawn around the nucleus of an atom to conceptualize where the electron might be located with the most probability. Heisenberg's uncertainty principle quantifies the inability to precisely locate the particle given its conjugate momentum. The typical model of the atom with a circular orbit around the nucleus has to be rethought in relation to quantum theory.

Quantum mechanics is also critically important for understanding how individual atoms combine covalently to form molecules and for understanding how the universe is interconnected with faster-than-light transfers of information.

By faith we understand that the worlds were set in order at God's command, so that the visible has its origin in the invisible. (Net Heb 11:3)

The existence and stability of atoms relies heavily on the fact that neutrons are slightly more massive than protons. The experimentally determined masses differ by only around 0.14 percent. A slightly smaller or larger value of the mass difference would lead to a dramatically different universe, with too many neutrons, not enough hydrogen, or too few heavier elements. This is a point of cosmic design showing an intelligent Creator. The tiny mass difference is the reason why free neutrons decay on average after around ten minutes, while protons -- the unchanging building blocks of matter -- remain stable for a practically unlimited period. Today, we know that protons and neutrons are composed of "up quarks" and "down quarks." The proton is made of one down and two up quarks, while the neutron is composed of one up and two down quarks. Most of the mass of the proton and neutron results from the energy carried by their quark constituents in accordance with Einstein's formula $E=mc2$.

Definition - In physics, quantum chromodynamics (QCD) is the theory of strong interactions, a fundamental force describing the interactions between quarks and gluons which make up hadrons such as the proton, neutron and pion.

Historical basis of quantum theory

"Quantum" comes from the Latin meaning "how much." It refers to the discrete units of matter and energy that are observed in quantum physics. At a fundamental level, both radiation and matter have characteristics of particles and waves. The recognition by scientists that radiation has particle-like properties and that matter has wavelike properties provided the impetus for the development of quantum mechanics. The birth of quantum physics is attributed to Max Planck in 1900. In 1897, J. J. Thomson who discovered the electron. Marie and Pierre Curie coined the term "radioactivity" to describe this property of matter, and isolated the radioactive elements radium and polonium. In 1911 Rutherford showed that the atom consists of a dense, positively charged nucleus surrounded by negatively charged electrons.

Quantum theory was accepted when the Compton Effect established that light carries momentum and can scatter off particles. When Louis de Broglie asserted that matter can be seen as behaving as a wave in much the same way as electromagnetic waves behave like particles (wave–particle duality)the Compton Effect was established.

An example, one very early experiment showed the wave form of particles was demonstrated by passing monochromatic light through a pair of slits. The two emerging beams interfere, so that a fringe pattern of alternately bright and dark bands appears on a screen. The bands are readily explained by a wave theory of light. According to the theory, a bright band is produced when the crests (and troughs) of the waves from the two slits arrive together at the screen. A dark band is produced when the crest of one wave arrives at the same time as the trough of the other, and the effects of the two light beams are canceled.

Quantum mechanics was extensively developed by Heisenberg, Wolfgang Pauli, Paul Dirac, and Erwin Schrödinger in 1926. Einstein used the quantum theory to explain the photoelectric effect, and in 1913 the Danish physicist Niels Bohr used the same constant to explain the stability and the frequencies of light emitted by hydrogen gas. The quantized theory of the atom gave way to a full-scale quantum mechanics in the 1920s. Since the 1970s, fundamental particle physics has provided insights into early universe cosmology, particularly the Big Bang theory proposed as a consequence of Einstein's general theory of relativity. *Given that God spoke the universe into existence it would appear as a big bang to an observer.*

Superstring Theory

Superstring theory is a hypothetical framework in which the point-like particles of particle physics are replaced by one-dimensional objects called strings. String theory aims to explain all types of observed rudimentary particles using quantum states of these strings. According to string theory, strings can vacillate in many ways. In addition to the particles hypothesized by the standard model of particle physics, string theory naturally incorporates gravity making it a candidate for a theory of everything. A TOE is a self-contained mathematical model that describes all fundamental forces and forms of matter.

Superstring theory postulates that there is a connection – a "supersymmetry" between bosons and a class of particles called fermions. Fermions include all quarks and leptons, as well as any composite particles made of an odd number of these, such as all baryons, many atoms, and nuclei. Examples of bosons include fundamental particles such as: photons, gluons, bosons, the Higgs boson, composite particles, and some quasiparticles such as Cooper pairs, plasmons, and phonons.

Superstring theory requires the existence of extra spatial dimensions for its mathematical uniformity. In genuine physical models constructed from string theory, these extra dimensions are stereotypically compacted to extremely small scales. Many theoretical physicists, including Stephen Hawking, believe that string theory is a step towards the correct fundamental description of nature.

String theory includes both open strings, which have two distinct endpoints, and closed strings, which form a complete loop. The two types of strings behave in slightly different ways, yielding different particle types. The motion of a point-like particle can be described by drawing a graph of its position with respect to time. The resulting picture depicts the worldline of the particle in spacetime. In an equivalent way, one can draw a graph representing the progress of a string as time passes. The string, which looks like a small line by itself, will sweep out a two-dimensional surface known as the worldsheet. A worldsheet is a two-dimensional manifold which describes the embedding of a string in spacetime. The different string modes give rise to different particles such as a photon which appear as a wave on this surface. A closed string looks like a small loop, so its worldsheet will look like a pipe. An open string looks like a segment with two endpoints, so its worldsheet will look like a strip.

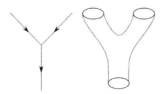

Strings can join and split.

In Superstring theory a **brane** (think another deminision) is a physical object that simplifies the notion of a point particle to higher dimensions. For example, a point particle can be viewed as a brane of dimension zero, while a string can be viewed as a brane of dimension one. It is also possible to consider higher-dimensional branes. The word brane comes from the word "membrane" which refers to a two-dimensional brane.

Branes are dynamical objects which can propagate through spacetime. They have mass and can have other attributes such as charge. Physicists often study fields corresponding to the electromagnetic field which live on the worldvolume of a brane. In Superstring theory, D-branes are an important class of branes that arise when one considers open strings. As an open string propagates through spacetime, its endpoints are required to lie on a D-brane. The letter "D" in D-brane refers to the fact that we impose a certain mathematical condition on the system known as the Dirichlet boundary condition. The study of D-branes in Superstring theory has led to important results.

Branes are frequently studied from a purely mathematical point of view. Mathematically, branes may be represented as objects of certain categories, such as the derived category of coherent sheaves on a Calabi–Yau manifold, or the Fukaya category.

The central idea is that the visible, four-dimensional universe (height, depth, length, and time) is restricted to a brane inside a higher-dimensional space. If the additional dimensions are compact, then the observed universe contains extra dimensions. Some versions of brane cosmology, based on extra dimensions, can explain the weakness of gravity relative to the other fundamental forces of nature, thus solving the so-called hierarchy problem. In the brane the other three forces (electromagnetism and the weak and strong nuclear forces) are localized on the brane (we live on a brane), but gravity has no such constraint and propagates on the full spacetime. Much of the gravitational power "leaks" into the other dimensions. As a consequence, the force of gravity should appear significantly stronger on small (subatomic) scales, where less gravitational force has "leaked". Various experiments are currently under way to test this. Extensions of the extra dimensions idea with supersymmetry in the bulk of dimensions appears to be promising in addressing the so-called cosmological constant problem thus linking Einstein's cosmology to quantum physics.

No discussion of Superstring theory would be complete without the mention of M-theory. M-theory is a theory in physics that unifies all consistent versions of superstring theory. M-theory would provide a framework for developing a unified theory of all of the fundamental forces of nature.

In everyday life, there are three familiar dimensions of space; height, width and length and we will add time. Hence, we have four dimensions. A notable feature of string theory and M-theory is that these theories require extra dimensions for their mathematical consistency. In string theory, spacetime is ten-dimensional, while in M-theory it is eleven-dimensional.

Calabi–Yau manifold.

M-theory provides a framework for constructing models of real world physics that combine general relativity with the standard model of particle physics. Typically, Superstring models are based on the idea of compactification (For this purpose it is assumed the extra dimensions are "wrapped" up on themselves, or "curled" up on Calabi–Yau spaces). Starting with the ten- or eleven-dimensional spacetime of string or M-theory, physicists postulate a shape for the extra dimensions. By choosing this shape appropriately, they can construct models roughly similar to the standard model of particle physics. One popular way of deriving realistic physics from string theory is to start with the heterotic theory in ten dimensions and assumes that the six extra dimensions of spacetime are shaped like a six-dimensional Calabi–Yau manifold. This is a special kind of geometric object named after mathematicians Eugenio Calabi and Shing-Tung Yau. Calabi–Yau manifolds offer many ways of extracting realistic physics from string theory.

.... and upholding all things by the word of his power... (Heb 1:3)

Theology

To the casual observer, the moment of creation might appear as a singularity or a big bang. This singularity was the result of having the realms compressed into words which the Lord spoke. Neither shadow nor illumination existed before creation. The Lord made this physical realm by mere will of having it appear, without any use of preexistent substance. Theologians refer to this as creatio ex nihilo, meaning "creation out of nothing." There are dimensions of reality without number (others that are incalculable). The realms were created out of the very substance and nature of God. I wrote in 2012 these words, "Many people are incapable of imagining other dimensions. But these dimensions are nevertheless real. A person cannot detect these other dimensions with their senses. However, mathematicians are beginning to understand because one way to think about other dimensions is to think in terms of circles which curl upon themselves and intertwine with time. The things seen and unseen consist of more than the few dimensions (of which we are aware). There are no fewer than ten dimensions, but I cannot describe what they look like or how one might approach an understanding of them. But suffice it to say they are beautiful and full of wonder! I can say this: one day humanity will transverse these dimensions, not at what we would call the speed of light, but faster, at the speed of thought. This will be during the time of restoration of all things in heaven and earth."

God and Jesus were in the beginning before "nothingness." Jesus created all things. Jesus is not a created being but was in existence with God before there was even an everlasting. *Logos* is Greek for *expression* or *utterance* and is defined by the passage itself in the fourteenth verse to be Jesus.

In the beginning was the Word (Logos-Jesus), and the Word was with God, and the **Word was God***. The same was in the beginning with God.* **All things were made by him** *(the Logos-Jesus); and without him was not any thing made that was made* (John 1:1–3).

The Big Bang

No book of this type would be complete without examining the "Big Bang" theory of cosmic evolution. One of the great problems for those who believe that the universe came into existence by itself is that the universe does not present itself in such a manner. The so-called 'Anthropic Principle' derives from the observation that many aspects of the universe have the appearance of having been designed specifically for human life. The complexity of quantum physics fits better with the idea that it has been specially created ex nihilo.

What is the Big Bang?

The Big Bang states that the universe expanded from a very high density and high temperature state, known as a singularity. And after the expansion, the universe cooled sufficiently to allow the formation of subatomic particles, atoms, and primordial elements to form stars and galaxies. In String Theory we would say that this "singularity" was caused by Banes coming in contact with one another.

"For in *him all things were created*: things in heaven and on earth, visible and invisible" Col. 1:16

So I would therefore say that God caused the Banes to contact one another. Specifically the spiritual world contacted another Bane causing the material world.

"Through faith we understand that the worlds were framed by the word of God, so that things which are seen were not made of things which do appear." Heb. 11:3

"Who serve unto the example and shadow of heavenly things, as Moses was admonished of God when he was about to make the tabernacle: for, See, saith he, that thou make all things according to the pattern shewed to thee in the mount." (Heb 8:5)

The material world is made like unto the pattern of the spiritual world. It was created during a singularity or contact with another Bane by the Word of God. The Big Bang or singularity didn't appear in space; rather, space began inside of the singularity. Prior to the singularity, nothing existed, not space, time, matter, or energy. Nothing excited, hence we from a Christian perspective would say ex nihilo.

The Atom Bomb

I have picked the Atom bomb to prove the point that had man known the principals of physics he could have built the bomb right outside the garden, because the Laws of Physics never change. They do not evolve.

The Little Boy bomb was dropped on Hiroshima and later Fat Man on Nagasaki ending the Second World War. While building the bombs scientists used what was known of physics to determine that the bombs would work. In fact the Laws of Physics are so ridged and unchanging that Little Boy was dropped without even being tested. They were sure it would work. *Why are the Laws of physics so ridged? Could they have happened by chance or through trial and error? Not a chance!*

Before we can get to the bomb, we have to start small. An atom you'll remember is made up of three larger subatomic particles **protons, neutrons** and **electrons**. The center of an atom, called the **nucleus**, is composed of protons and neutrons (nucleons). The mass number is the number of protons and neutrons both of which are called baryons. This is not the same as the atomic number which denotes the number of protons in a nucleus, and thus uniquely identifying it as an element. Protons and electrons have opposite charges and therefore attract one another. Electrons orbit around the nucleus. The proton-to-electron ratio is always one to one, so the atom as a whole has a neutral charge unless it is ionized (stripped of its electrons). Hydrogen has one proton, one neutron, and one electron. A water molecule is made from two hydrogen atoms and one oxygen atom bound together into a single unit called a molecule. However, if you change the number of protons, you wind up with a different element altogether. If you alter the number of neutrons in an atom, you wind up with an **isotope**. If you take an atom of hydrogen and put it in a bottle and come back in several million years, it will still be an atom of hydrogen. Hydrogen is therefore called a **stable** atom.

Certain elements have isotopes that are **radioactive or unstable**. Isotopes are variants of a particular chemical element which differ in neutron number, although all isotopes of a given element have the same number of protons in each atom. Hydrogen is a good example of an element with multiple isotopes, one of which is radioactive. Normal hydrogen, protium, has one proton and no neutrons. There is another isotope, deuterium (heavy water) which has one proton and one neutron. Deuterium is very rare in nature. It acts like protium (for example, you can make water out of it) it turns out it is different enough from protium in that it is toxic in high concentrations. The deuterium isotope of hydrogen is stable. A third isotope, tritium, has one proton and two neutrons. It turns out this isotope is **unstable (radioactive)**. That is, if you have a container full of tritium (half-life of 12 ½ years) and come back in a million years, you will find that it has all turned into helium-3 (two protons, one neutron), which is stable. The process by which it turns into helium is called **radioactive decay.**

The existence of deuterium at a low but constant primordial fraction in all hydrogen is another one of the arguments in favor of the Big Bang theory over the Steady State theory of the universe.

Nuclear fission was discovered in 1938. In this reaction, a neutron plus a fissionable atom causes a fission resulting in a larger number of neutrons than the single one that was consumed in the initial reaction. Thus was born the bomb. A nuclear reaction is considered to be the process in which two nuclei, or else a nucleus of an atom and a subatomic particle (such as a proton, neutron, or high energy electron) from outside the atom, collide to produce one or more nuclides that are different from the nuclide that began the process.

Fission is a form of nuclear transmutation because the resulting fragments are not the same element as the original atom. The two nuclei produced are most often of comparable but slightly different sizes, typically with a mass ratio of products of about 3 to 2, for common fissile isotopes. Most often produced is krypton 85 (10 year half-life) and 92 (half-life 1.48 seconds) and barium 141 (14 year half-life).

Certain elements have naturally radioactive isotopes. Uranium is the best example of such an element. The primary natural isotopes of uranium are uranium-235 (0.7 percent), which is fissile, and uranium-238 (99.3 percent), which is fissionable (it can combine with atoms at high heat and pressure such as in a fission bomb) but not fissile. In nature, plutonium exists only in minute concentrations, so the fissile isotope plutonium-239 is made artificially in nuclear reactors from uranium-238.

Uranium is heavy, lighter only than plutonium. Its density is about 70% higher than that of lead. It occurs naturally in low concentrations of a few parts per million in soils, rock and water, and is commercially extracted from uranium-bearing minerals such as uraninite. A pound of highly enriched uranium 235 as used to power a nuclear reactor is equal to about a million gallons of gasoline. Highly enriched uranium (70%) is called oralloy.

In an atomic bomb or nuclear reactor, first a small number of uranium-235 neutrons (or plutonium-239) is given enough energy to collide with some fissionable uranium-235, which in turn produces additional free neutrons. A portion of these neutrons are captured by nuclei that do not fission. Others escape the material without being captured (we will talk about dampers later); and the remainder cause further fissions. This continuing process whereby neutrons emitted by fissioning uranium-235 and by inducing of other fissions in other uranium-235 nuclei we call a chain reaction. If the number of fissions in one generation is equal to the number of neutrons in the preceding generation, the system is said to be critical; if the number is greater than one, it is supercritical; and if it is less than one, it is subcritical. In the case of a nuclear reactor, the number of fissionable nuclei available in each generation is carefully controlled to prevent a "runaway" chain reaction. In the case of an atomic bomb, however, a very rapid growth in the number of fissions is sought. Fission weapons are normally made with materials having high concentrations of the fissile isotopes uranium-235, plutonium-239, or some combination of these.

The minimum mass of fissile material necessary to sustain a chain reaction is called the critical mass. This quantity depends on the type, density, and shape of the fissile material and the degree to which surrounding materials reflect neutrons back into the fissile core. A mass that is less than the critical amount is said to be subcritical, while a mass greater than the critical amount is referred to as supercritical. The atomic bomb dropped on Hiroshima, Japan, in 1945, contained only about 140 pounds of highly enriched uranium; however it released energy equaling about 15 kilotons of TNT. However, only about 1.6 pounds fissioned. Modern bombs

(B-83) may be as large as 75 times the yield of the atomic bomb dropped on Hiroshima.

In order to make an explosion, fission weapons do not require pure uranium or plutonium. Most of the uranium used in current US nuclear weapons is approximately 93.5 percent enriched uranium-235. Plutonium weapons typically contain 93 percent plutonium-239. It is thought that Little Boy, the first nuclear weapon used in war as only 70%-80% enriched. Although theoretically for an implosion design, a minimum of 20% could be sufficient. It would require hundreds of kilograms of material and would not be a practical design for a country. However, for a "truck" bomb this just might work. Hence, you must see the danger of Iran today. Iran already has uranium enriched to 70%. It is also known that 95% of the energy required to enrich uranium is spent on the first 70%, not the last 10% or 15%.

In order to produce a nuclear explosion, subcritical masses of fissionable material must be rapidly assembled into a supercritical configuration. The simplest weapon design is the pure fission gun-assembly device, in which an explosive propellant is used to fire one subcritical mass down a "gun barrel" into another subcritical mass (Little Boy). Therefore, gun-assembly weapons are made with highly enriched uranium, typically more than 80 percent uranium-235. Plutonium cannot be used as the fissile material in a gun-assembly device, because the speed of assembly in this device is too slow to preclude the high probability that a chain reaction will "pre-initiate" (fizzle) by spontaneous neutron emission, thereby generating an explosive yield of only a few tens of tons. Little Boy had a muzzle velocity of 980 feet per second, much too slow for the implosion method to work. An example

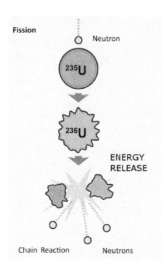

was once given by a professor that were you to have two subcritical masses of uranium 235 in your hands that before you could put your hands together they would "fizzle" and the room would explode causing and a large amount of radioactivity to be released. But, this would not create a "bomb" type of explosion.

Picture this - A neutron is absorbed by a uranium 335 nucleus, turning it briefly into an excited uranium-236 nucleus. Then the uranium-236 splits into fast-moving lighter elements (fission products) and releases three free neutrons. This is a chain reaction. Subatomic particles collide with an atomic nucleus and cause changes to it. Chain reactions are thus driven by the mechanics of bombardment. In such a reaction, free neutrons released by each fission event can trigger yet more events, which in turn release more neutrons and cause more fission. When fission is uncontrolled it is the basis of the atomic bomb. Controlled fission is the basis of nuclear power. In a rector fission is controlled by moderators called control rods which start and stop the fission process. In the bomb the effort is made to control the fission only long enough to expedite the explosion. There are several ways this is accomplished and we will talk about them later.

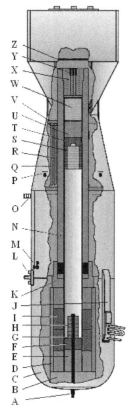

Little Boy showing major mechanical component placement. Drawing is shown to scale. Numbers in ( ) indicate quantity of identical components. Not shown are the APS-13 radar units, clock box with pullout wires, baro switches and tubing, batteries, and electrical wiring.

Z) Armor Plate
Y) Mark XV electric gun primers (3)
X) Gun breech with removable inner plug
W) Cordite powder bags (4)
V) Gun tube reinforcing sleeve
U) Projectile steel back
T) Projectile Tungsten-Carbide disk
S) U-235 projectile rings (9)
R) Alignment rod (3)
Q) Armored tube containing primer wiring (3)
P) Baro ports (8)
O) Electrical plugs (3)
N) 6.5" bore gun tube
M) Safing/arming plugs (3)
L) Lift lug
K) Target case gun tube adapter
J) Yagi antenna assembly (4)
I) Four-section 13" diameter Tungsten-Carbide tamper cylinder sleeve
H) U-235 target rings (6)
G) Polonium-Beryllium initiators (4)
F) Tungsten-Carbide tamper plug
E) Impact absorbing anvil
D) K-46 steel target liner sleeve
C) Target case forging
B) 15" diameter steel nose plug forging
A) Front nose locknut attached to 1" diameter main steel rod holding target components

Beryllium neutron sources, named urchin neutron initiators (beryllium pellet, and a beryllium shell with polonium between the two), were used in the Little Boy, but not in modern weapons. Inside the Little Boy, the uranium-235 was divided into two parts, following the gun principle: the "projectile" and the "target". The projectile was a hollow cylinder with 60% of the total mass 85 lbs. It consisted of a stack of 9 uranium rings, each 6.25-inch in diameter with a 4-inch bore in the center, and a total length of 7 inches, pressed together into the front end of a thin-walled projectile 16.25 inches long. Filling in the remainder of the space behind these rings in the projectile was a tungsten carbide disc with a steel back. At ignition, the projectile slug was pushed 42 inches along a 72-inch long, 6.5-inch cannon barrel. The slug was a 4 inch cylinder, 7 inches in length with a 1 inch axial hole. The slug comprised 40% of the total fissile mass uranium-235 at 56 lbs. The insert was a stack of 6 washer-like uranium discs somewhat thicker than the projectile rings that were slid over a 1 inch rod. This rod then extended forward through the tungsten carbide tamper plug, impact-absorbing anvil, and nose plug backstop eventually protruding out the front of the bomb casing.

When the hollow-front projectile reached the target and slid over the target insert, the assembled super-critical mass of uranium was completely surrounded by a damper and neutron reflector of tungsten carbide and steel, both materials having a combined weight of 5,100 lbs. Neutron initiators at the base of the projectile were activated by the impact. The reaction might have been moderated by uranium in the outer casing, or beryllium as was used in Fat Man.

The other major assembly method is implosion (Fat Man) in which a sphere (a hollow sphere is the perfect shape for a fissile core) having the fewest escaping neutrons per unit of material. This shape allows for the smallest critical mass. The critical mass of a base sphere of uranium-235 at normal density is approximately 104 pounds; for plutonium-239, a base critical mass is 22 pounds. However, the critical mass can be lowered in several ways, the most common being surrounding the sphere with some other material that reflects some of the escaping neutrons back into the fissile core (such a uranium 239 and/or beryllium). Practical reflectors can reduce the critical mass by a factor of two or three, so that about 15 kg (33 pounds) of uranium-235 and about 5 to 10 kg (11 to 22 pounds) of either plutonium-239 or uranium-233 at normal density can become critical. The critical mass can also be lowered by compressing the fissile core, because at higher densities emitted neutrons are more likely to strike a fissionable nucleus before escaping. Thin plates or foils of beryllium are sometimes used in nuclear weapon designs as the very outer layer of the plutonium pits in the primary stages of thermonuclear bombs, placed to surround the fissile material. These layers of beryllium are good "pushers" for the implosion of the plutonium-239, and they are also good neutron reflectors. In the simplest design, a spherical fissile core is surrounded by a reflector or tamper, which in turn is surrounded by the chemical high explosive and an air space. To obtain a given yield, considerably less fissile material is needed for an implosion weapon than for a gun-assembly device. An implosion fission weapon with an explosive yield of one kiloton can be constructed with as little as 2.2 to 4.4 pounds of plutonium or with 11 to 22 pounds of highly enriched uranium.

Why, because all of physics operate within "laws." These laws have never changed and are predictable to the point of being able to be used to create a bomb. I see Divine inspiration in the set pattern of physics. The laws don't change.

With no evolution on the quantum physics level how can you have evolution on the physical level? Hence, creationism is proven.

Natural Fission Reactor

A natural nuclear fission reactor was discovered in 1972 at Oklo in Gabon, Africa. It is a uranium deposit where self-sustaining nuclear chain reactions have occurred naturally. Self-sustaining nuclear fission reactions took place approximately 1.7 billion years ago, and ran for a few hundred thousand years, averaging 100 kW of thermal power during that time.

The natural reactor of Oklo has been used to check if the atomic fine-structure constant α (also known as Sommerfeld's constant, commonly denoted α- is a fundamental physical constant characterizing the strength of the electromagnetic interaction between elementary charged particles) could have changed over the past 2 billion years? It is important because α influences the rate of various nuclear reactions. For example, Samarium-149 captures a neutron to become Samarium-150, and since the rate of neutron capture depends on the value of α, the ratio of the two samarium isotopes in samples from Oklo can be used to calculate the value of the atomic fine-structure constant α from 2 billion years ago. Several studies have analyzed the relative concentrations of radioactive isotopes left behind at Oklo, and most have concluded that nuclear reactions then were much the same as they are today, implying that the atomic fine-structure constant α was the same then as it is now. Hence, the laws of physics have not changed since the Earth was created. This destroys any idea that the laws of physics change over time. No evolution on the quantum physics level. ***With no evolution on the quantum physics level, how can there be evolution on the physical level?***

How do we then explain the great age of the Earth? By an understanding what is called Ruin-Recreationism. The Earth was created 4.5 billion years ago, but suffered destruction between Genesis verse one and two, because we find the Earth is "without form and void" in the second verse. The other verses use a Hebrew word which the KJV translates as "made" it is "aw-saw" and it means to make out of something that already exists. Genesis 1:1, the word created is "baw-raw" and means to create out of nothing. After Genesis 1:1 the word "made" is used instead of (the word) create. Aw-saw is translated as made instead of create so the reader knows it is a different assertion. Hence, the six days of Genesis are the account of a re-creation, or regeneration, of a previously existent heavens and earth, (not the original creation). And the seven creative days within Genesis Chapter 1 are not a geological history of the earth!

The science behind both Carbon and Argon data is flawed, but not by millions of years. Carbon and Argon dating based upon radioactive decay may have been accelerated in the recent past. However, the vast age assigned to the earth based on radioactive measurements can by no means be set aside.

Thus, Ruin-Restoration Creationism best fits the overall understanding of the creative acts of God. In summary, God existed. He created the earth perfectly (Genesis1:1), but it became a wasteland because of war in the heavens (Genesis 1:2). God then remade the earth out of the old materials of the previous creation in a literal six-day period. Ruin-Restoration Creationism proves that the Biblical story of creation is in harmony with the teachings of modern science, and this casts a new light on the integrity of the Bible.

Creation

To some scientists, the moment of creation might appear as a singularity or a big bang.

This singularity was the result of having the realms -branes compressed into God's spoken Word. These words exploded into the worlds we see now, the realms-branes we don't see, and the rudiments and stones of fire (worlds). Neither shadow nor illumination existed before creation. The Lord made this physical realm by mere act of will having it appear, without any use of preexistent substance. Theologians refer to this as creatio ex nihilo, meaning "creation out of nothing." There are dimensions of reality without number and dimensions that cannot be calculated. The realms were created out of the very substance and nature of God. We are all in this manner His children because of this creative act. We had preexistence within the mind of God.

The Lord lives in a realm which has no beginning and no end. Because He is in a timeless present, His perspective sees our past, present, and future as a present happening.

He is uniquely positioned to judge all things because He sees what is happening everywhere in the different realms at any time, in history present, past, or future.

There are many dimensions, some of which exist alongside this dimension.

Many people are incapable of imagining other dimensions. But these dimensions are real nevertheless. A person cannot detect these other dimensions with their senses. However, mathematicians are beginning to understand because they think about other dimensions in terms of circles which curl upon themselves and intertwine with time (aka) Calabi–Yau spaces.

The things seen and unseen consist of more than the few dimensions of which we are aware. There are no fewer than eleven dimensions, but I cannot describe what they look like or tell you how you might approach an understanding of them. But suffice it to say they are beautiful and full of wonder!

I can tell you this: one day humanity will transverse these dimensions, not at the speed of light, but faster: at the speed of thought.

This will take place during the time of restoration of all things in heaven and earth.

Looking for and hasting unto the coming of the day of God, wherein the heavens being on fire shall be dissolved, and the elements shall melt with fervent heat? Nevertheless we, according to his promise, look for new heavens and a new earth, wherein dwelleth righteousness. (2Pe 3:12-13)

Let's look at how angels travel, for this will be important later. They simply *will* themselves to be somewhere, and they are there. They have no sense of traveling, no sense of boundaries. There are no walls to impede their movement.

Let me offer a simple explanation: an angel can be at any moment in the center of a circle or move in any direction and remain equidistant to every point around the circle's circumference at any given moment of time.

God and Jesus were in the beginning before "nothingness." Jesus created all things. Jesus is not a created being but was rather in existence with God before there was even an everlasting. *Logos* is Greek for *expression* or *utterance* and is defined by the passage itself in the fourteenth verse to be Jesus.

> *In the beginning was the Word (Logos-Jesus), and the Word was with God, and the **Word was God**. The same was in the beginning with God. **All things were made by him** (the Logos-Jesus); and without him was not any thing made that was made* (John 1:1–3).

The essence of the argument for design is that highly regimented phenomena (such as Quantum physics) demonstrates a complexity that cannot be explained through natural causes; it requires creation by an "intelligent agent" God himself.

Author's Biography

I was born in a small, insignificant town in the southern part of the US, so far south that they had to pipe in the sunshine! I was born in the month of April into a family of twelve in South Georgia on an island called Cumberland. April, in the south, warms as it recovers from mild winters and takes on a new life as azaleas bloom, porpoises frolic, and wild horses give birth to new colts. Cumberland is a wonderful place with its tidal pools, abundant wildlife, untouched sand dunes, deep forests, and history. (Heck, around the turn of the century, we even had a bear!). I will not mention the alligators, other than to say we had our share of them, but they are about as worthless as the sharks, of which Christmas Creek has an ample supply. My siblings and I explored the beaches and the forests on a daily basis.

Each of us learned to swim at the ripe young age of five by being thrown off the dock with a rope tied around the waist. Our father thought it was of the utmost importance that we learn to swim. I guess he was right, seeing that we lived on an island! Perhaps the training method was a little harsh (I would not recommend it), but it was effective.

Somewhere around the time I had reached eight or so years of age, I experienced my first vision. One evening, as I returned to my bedroom, a wall disappeared. Where the wall had been was a man sitting upon a stage. He sat in a chair at the edge of the stage, putting his hands upon the heads of those passing by beneath him. As I watched these people walk beneath him, he laid his hands upon them. I realized that the man was me, just older! It was obvious that I was in some kind of ministry. I thought all of this very unusual, because I had never seen anything like it. All I knew about ministry at this time was what I learned in the Methodist church. You can rest assured nothing like this was going on in the Methodist church in the 1960s!

I was, by definition, a tenacious child, but about what, I did not know. In the early 1970s, upon turning twelve, I took my first steps into business ownership; I built a shop in my parents' backyard and began repairing lawnmowers. It was a great income for a teenager, perhaps too good.

As with most coming-of-age young people, sin lurked at my doorstep, and by 1977, I was an aspiring teenage alcoholic, complete with blackouts. Even at this tender age, the world had shown its web of deceit, lies, and drama.

I will always be indebted to a caring science teacher, whose name has been lost to time, for his introducing me to the living Christ. As most of us have heard of Christ, I had heard, having grown up, as I mentioned, in church. However, this humble man was the first person I had met who really seemed to have a relationship with this Jesus, the God-man. I am sure there must have been other people like him with whom I had contact, but none that I knew seemed to have the kind of feelings exemplifying a real relationship with Jesus. I began to talk with him between classes. On one particular day, I meditated on a text of Scripture in Ecclesiastes.

> *Vanity of vanities, saith the Preacher, vanity of vanities; all is vanity* (Ecclesiastes 1:2).

I was moved by a war of sorts that seemed to be going on within me; it was as if evil was determined to drag my soul along with it. Evil was literally vying within me for my soul and it had the opposite effect. You could say that it scared the hell out of me. I returned the next day to talk again with my teacher. I eagerly waited for the class to end, knowing I then would have time to speak about the struggle I had felt the night before in my soul. When the moment arrived, I dashed from my desk to where he stood.

I began to relate the struggle I had felt, and he asked me if I would pray and receive Christ. I wanted to, but could not speak. I had become dumb; I was not able to open my mouth to speak in any manner! Seeming to understand this strange occurrence, he pointed directly at me and spoke commandingly to a devil, one that I could not see. He told the devil to go, in the name of Jesus! Immediately, I cried at the top of my voice, "JESUS!"

I knew not what to say, only crying out to Jesus, the one I knew who, alone, could rescue me from the war that had only moments ago rendered me unable to speak. As I heard myself cry out, I became aware of the darkness within my soul. It was as if I was looking inside of myself as some kind of spectator.

As I surveyed the vastness of this darkness, I became cognizant of the fact that in the middle of this vast darkness, there was a pinpoint of light beginning to expand. This happened at an ever-increasing velocity until it appeared as a supernova and burst forth out of every part of my being, leaving my extremities at what seemed to me, to be the speed of light. I staggered a few feet and recovered my composure; I was stunned.

I certainly had no point of reference for what I had just experienced. The years to come would, of course, show the vast changes that had occurred. I no longer was an alcoholic or an addict of any kind from that moment forward. I later learned that the old man had died and the new man had been born. I had been born again and would never be the same. Now, nearly four decades later, I can say it was the defining moment of my life.

If you have enjoyed this book, or it has had an impact on your life, we would like to hear from you.

****

Dr. CK Quarterman is available to speak at your function, church group, or meeting on any Bible subject. If you would like him to join your discussion by phone, please include that in your request. He would be more than happy to join you for an hour by conference line. Appointments are set on a first-come basis, and depend on availability.

For more information about Dr. CK Quarterman and his books, please visit:

Website: http://www.ckquarterman.com/

Email - ckquarter@gmail.com

FB: http://www.facebook.com/ckquarter

Our mission is to alert and awaken the world that is hoping for a better tomorrow. The end is near, America is failing, and the footfall of the Apocalypse's Four Horsemen is on the doorstep. Our objective is to embolden those who are in need of more than the Sunday sermon, remove the roadblocks so they can advance as well as embrace the truth of the hour in which we live, and prepare everyone for Christ's imminent return.

Please visit:

http://www.deliveranceministriesgroup.com/

http://www.endtimeministrieschurch.com

http://www.fallenangelstoday.com/

http://www.theislamicantichrist.com/

Books by Dr. CK Quarterman

The Watchers

Fallen Angels UFO's and The New World Order

Revelation: Know the End

Three Days and Nights to Glory

Quantum Physics & Intelligent design

Marriage a Covenant

Islamic Antichrist

Printed in Great Britain
by Amazon

23961253R10036